Ask Nurse Pfaff, She'll Help You!

written by
ALICE K. FLANAGAN

photographs by
CHRISTINE OSINSKI

Reading Consultant
LINDA CORNWELL
Learning Resource Consultant
Indiana Department of Education

CHILDREN'S PRESS® *A Division of Grolier Publishing*
New York • London • Hong Kong • Sydney • Danbury, Connecticut

Special thanks to Barbara Pfaff
for allowing us to tell her story.

Also, thanks to the Staten Island
University Hospital.

Author's note:
Nurse Pfaff's last name is pronounced FAFF.

Library of Congress Cataloging-in-Publication Data
Flanagan, Alice.
    Ask Nurse Pfaff, she'll help you! / written by Alice K. Flanagan ;
photographs by Christine Osinski ; reading consultant, Linda Cornwell.
      p. cm. — (Our neighborhood)
    Summary: Simple text and photographs describe the work of a
nurse taking care of patients at a hospital.
    ISBN 0-516-20495-5 (lib.bdg.)   0-516-26208-4 (pbk.)
    1. Nurses—Juvenile literature. [1. Nurses. 2. Occupations.] I.
Osinski, Christine, ill. II. Title. III. Series: Our neighborhood.
RT61.5.F53 1997
610.73—dc21

                                         97-4127
                                           CIP
                                           AC

Photographs ©: Christine Osinski

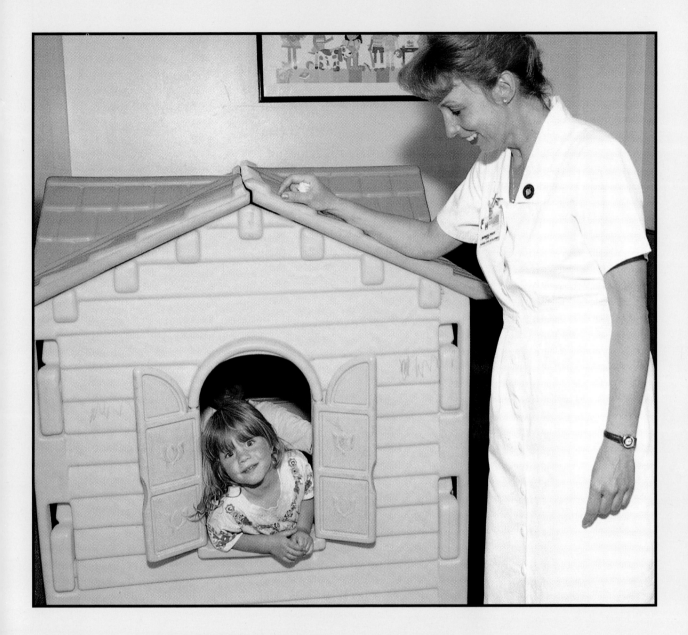

In our hospital, there is a very
special nurse. Her name is
Nurse Pfaff.

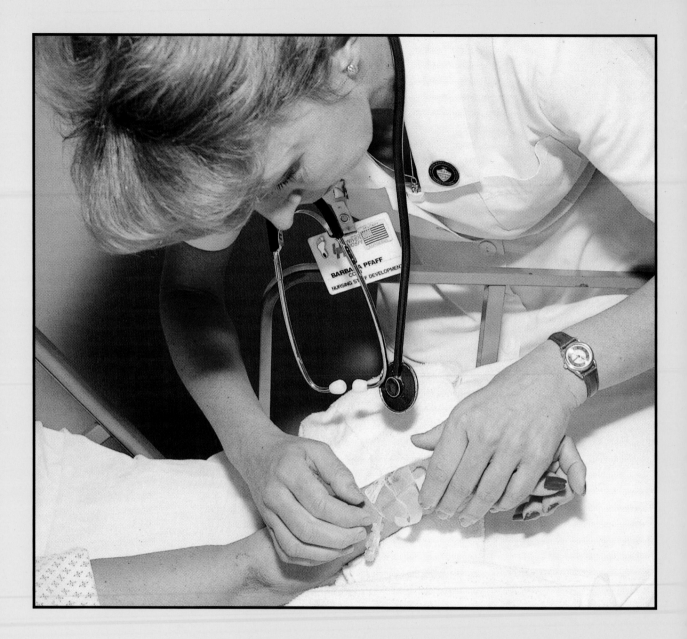

She is kind and gentle with people.

And she's dependable. She's always there when patients need her.

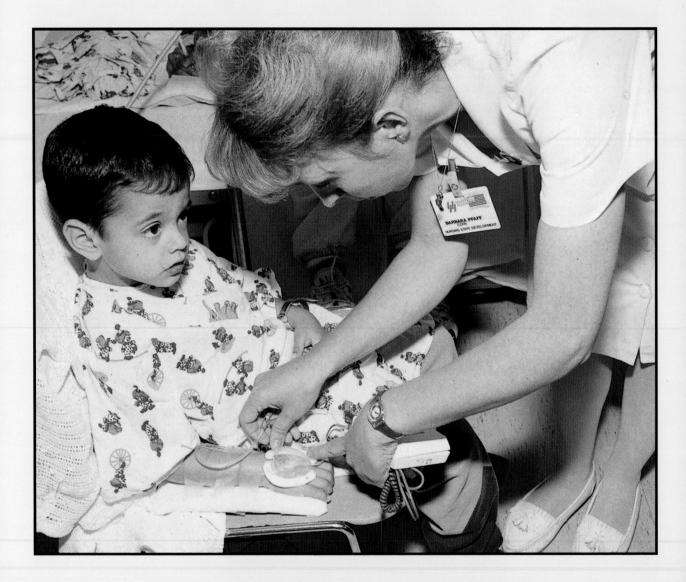

Nurse Pfaff cares for everyone—the young and the old.

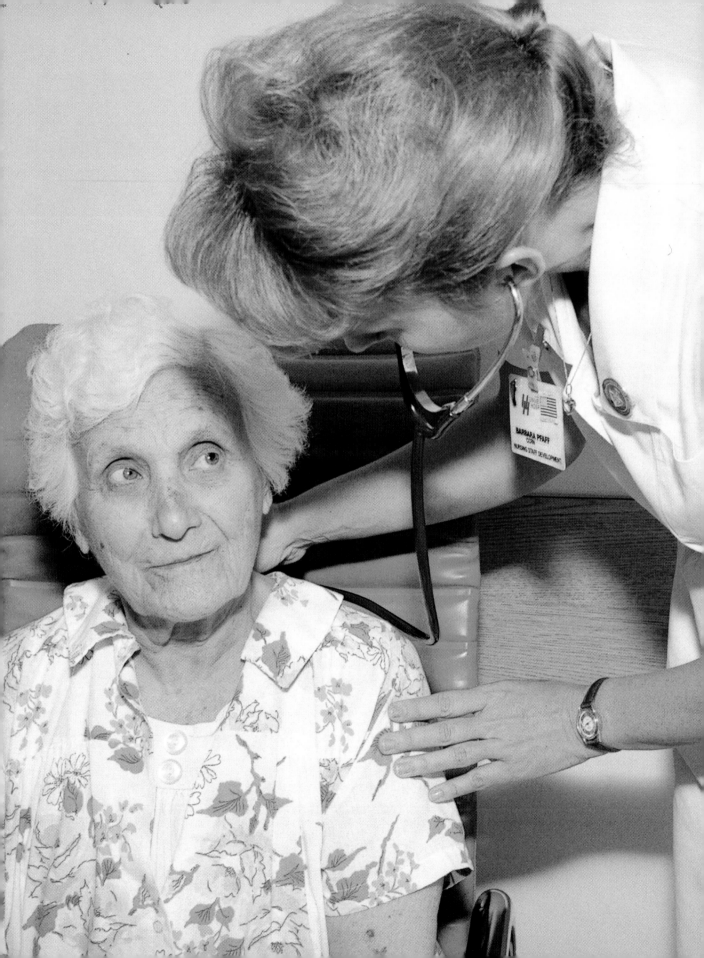

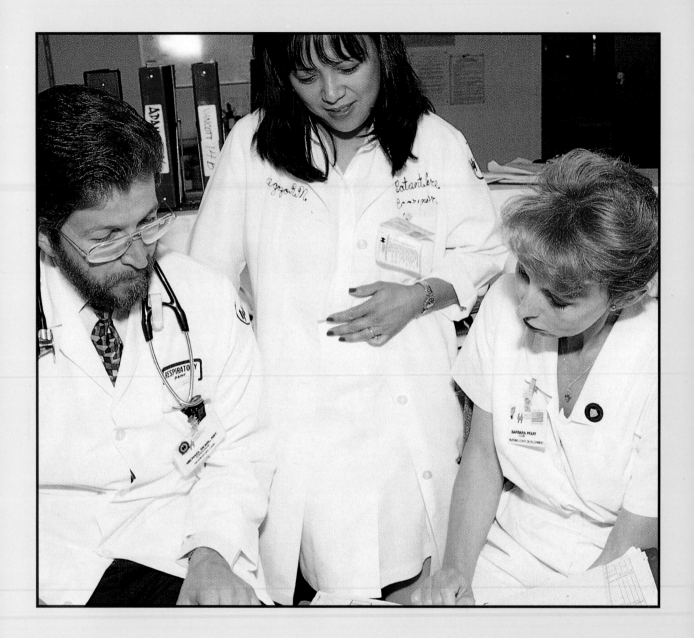

She helps doctors take care of people
who are sick . . .

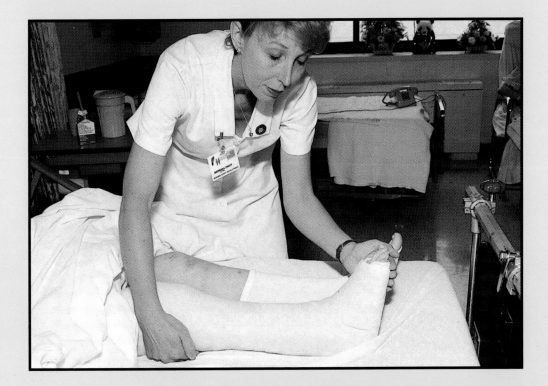

. . . or have broken bones.

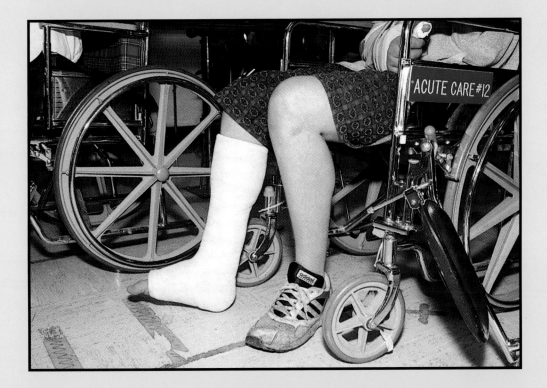

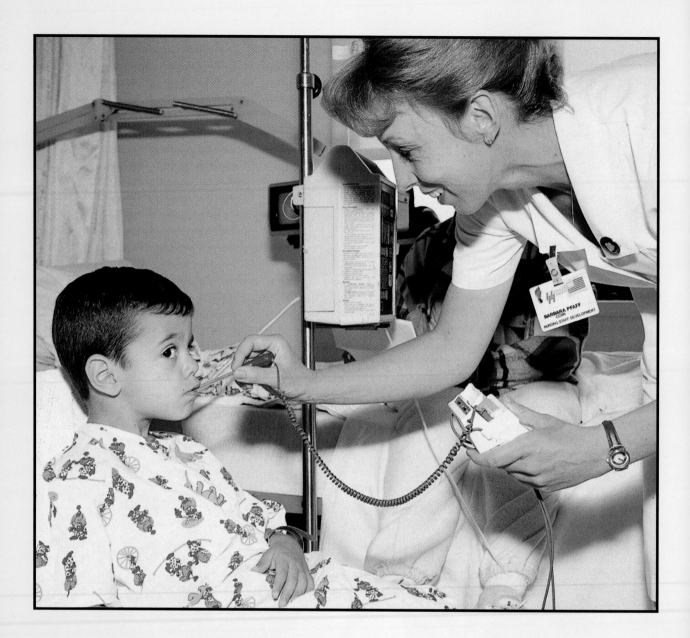

At her job, Nurse Pfaff uses many tools, such as a thermometer

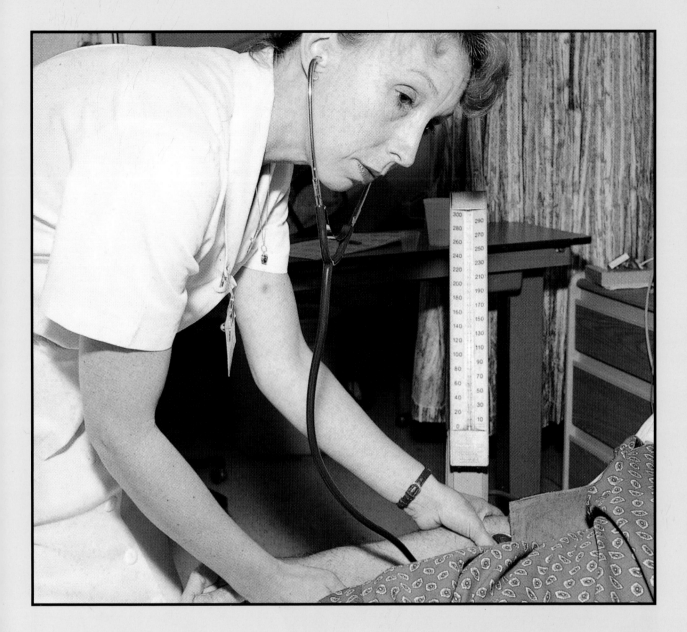

and a stethoscope.

She could not do her job without a blood-pressure cuff

or a scale that shows how much people weigh.

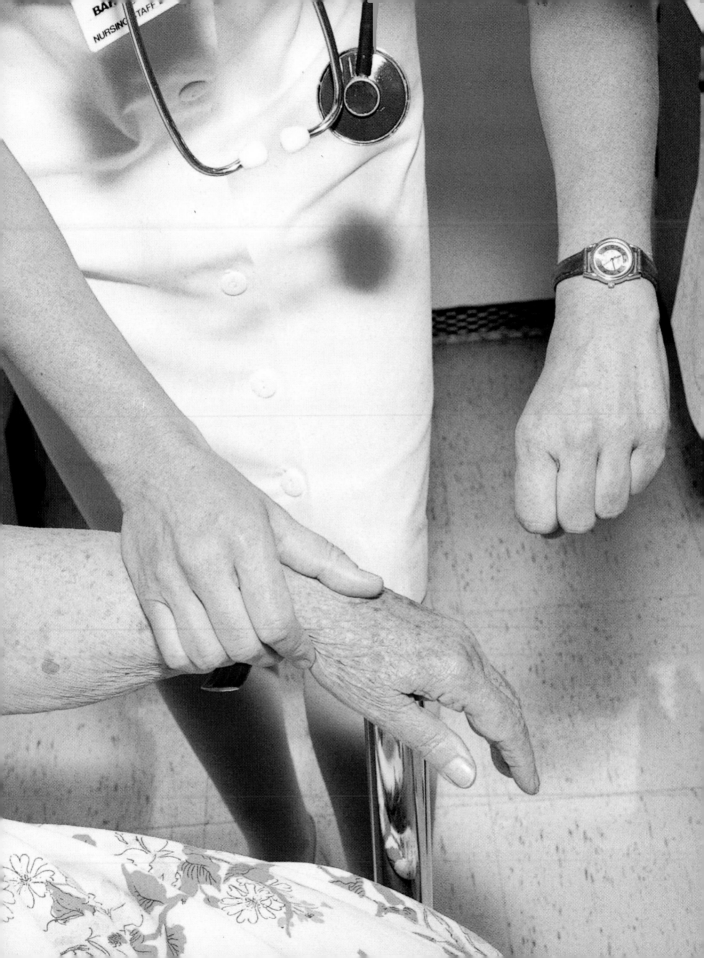

A watch keeps Nurse Pfaff on time. With it, she can tell how fast a patient's heart is beating, or when it's time to give someone medicine.

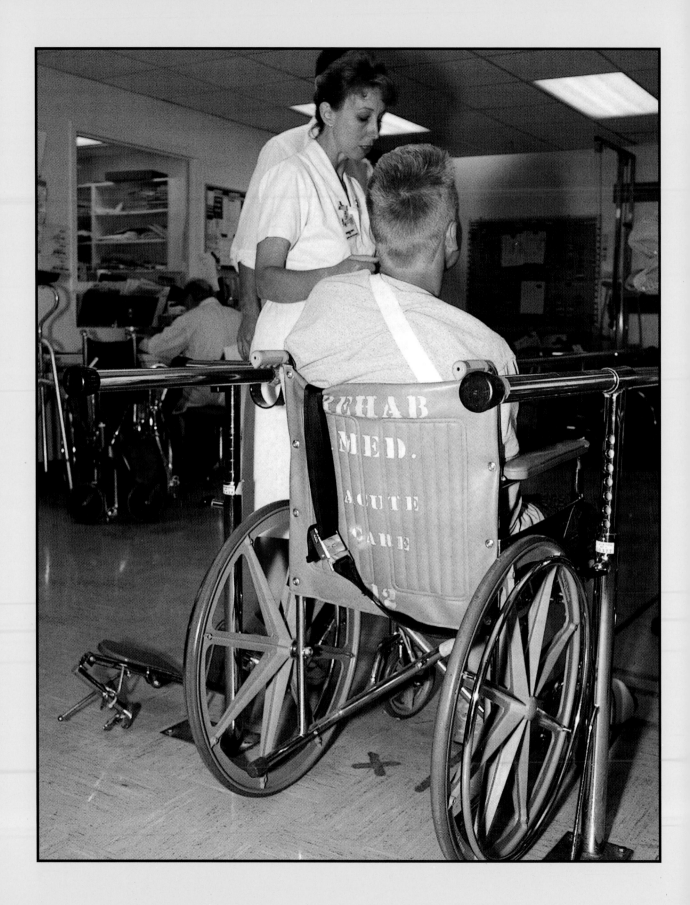

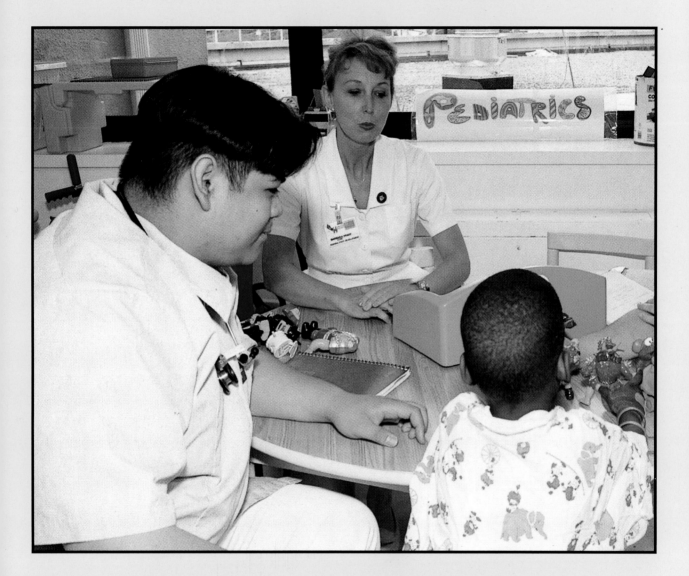

Of all the things Nurse Pfaff does,
teaching people how to get better is
what she likes most.

Sometimes, she teaches with pictures and charts.

Sometimes,
she uses a
puppet for fun!

Each day she writes a lot
of reports. A nurse's job
is never done.

21

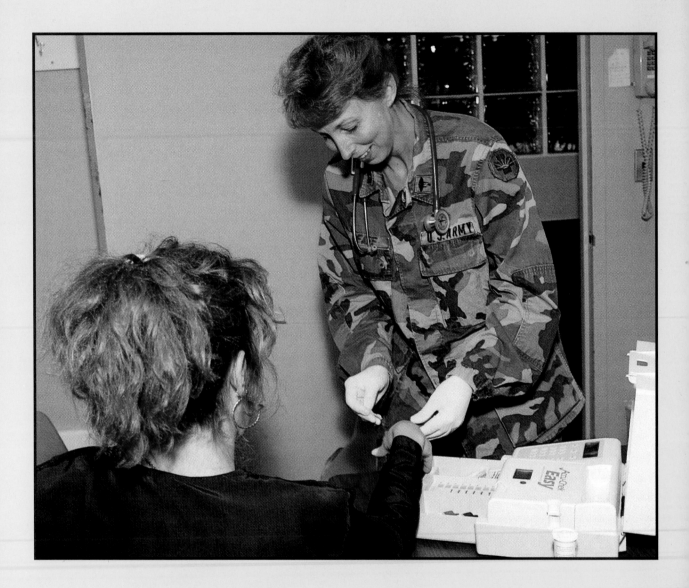

Nurse Pfaff works at another job, too. She's a captain in the United States Army.

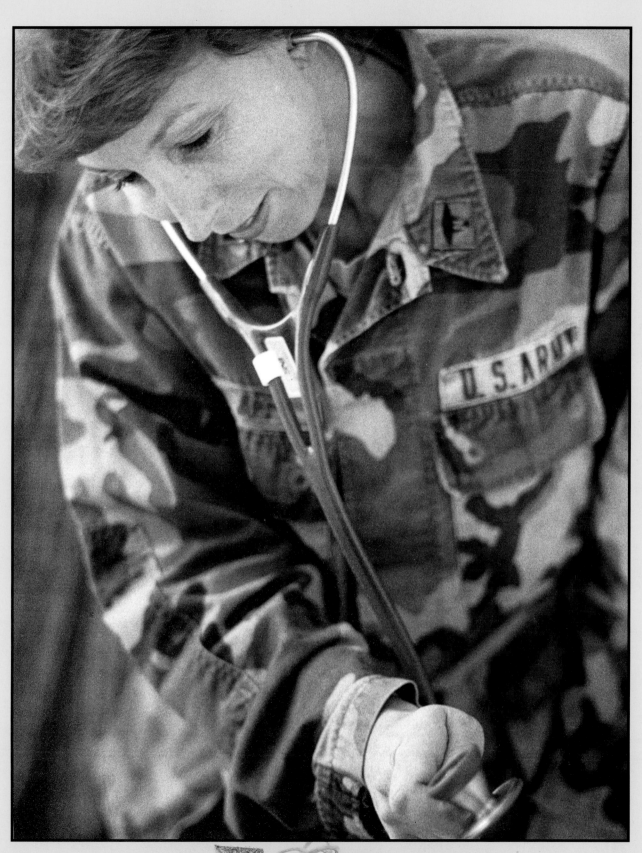

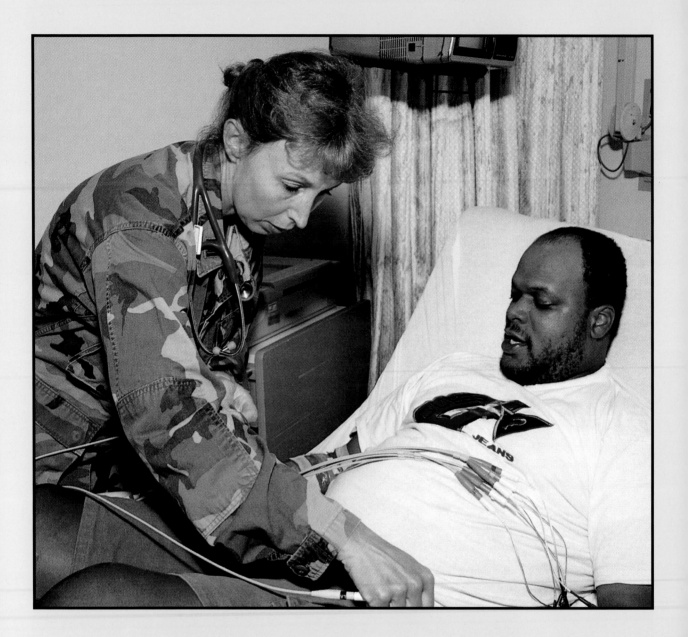

Captain Pfaff cares for soldiers who are sick or hurt.

She will go to war if her country needs her.

Being a nurse is very hard work, because a hospital stays open every day of the year. Sometimes, patients die. Then it's a sad time for everyone.

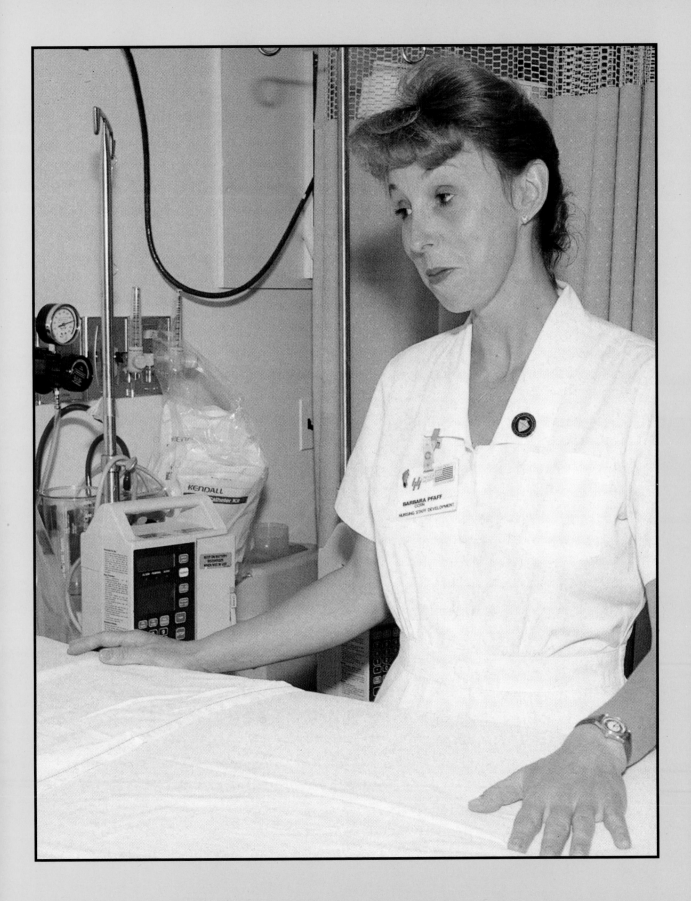

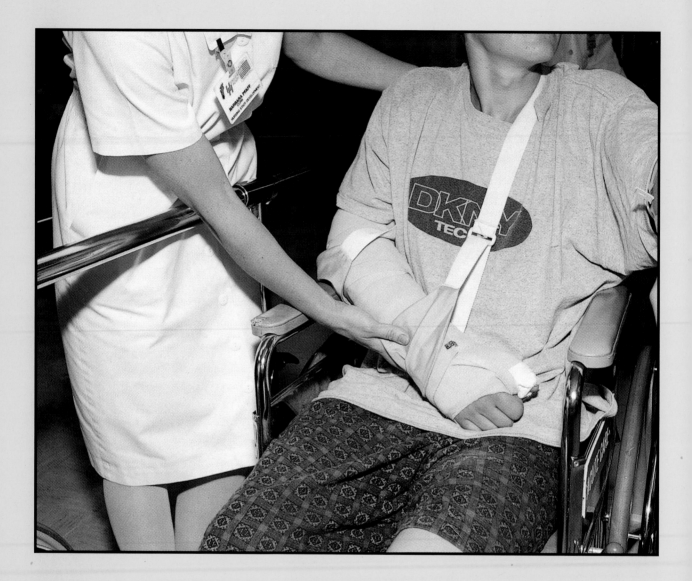

Nurse Pfaff loves helping people.
It makes her feel good.

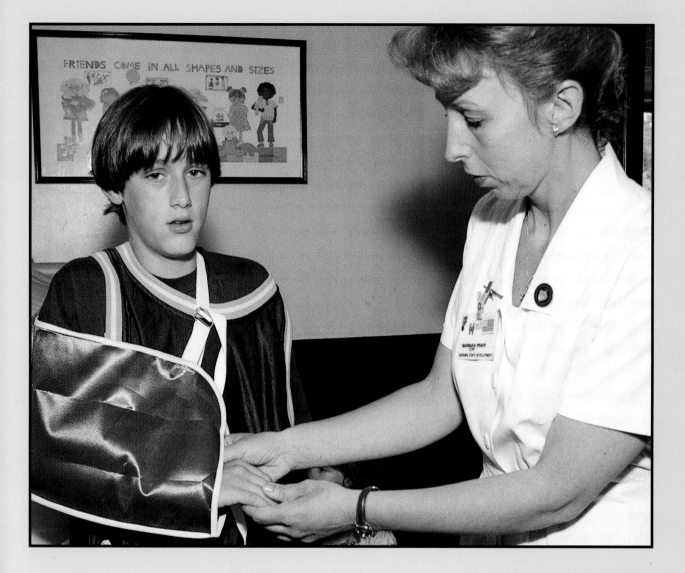

Even when she's tired, she never
turns anyone away.

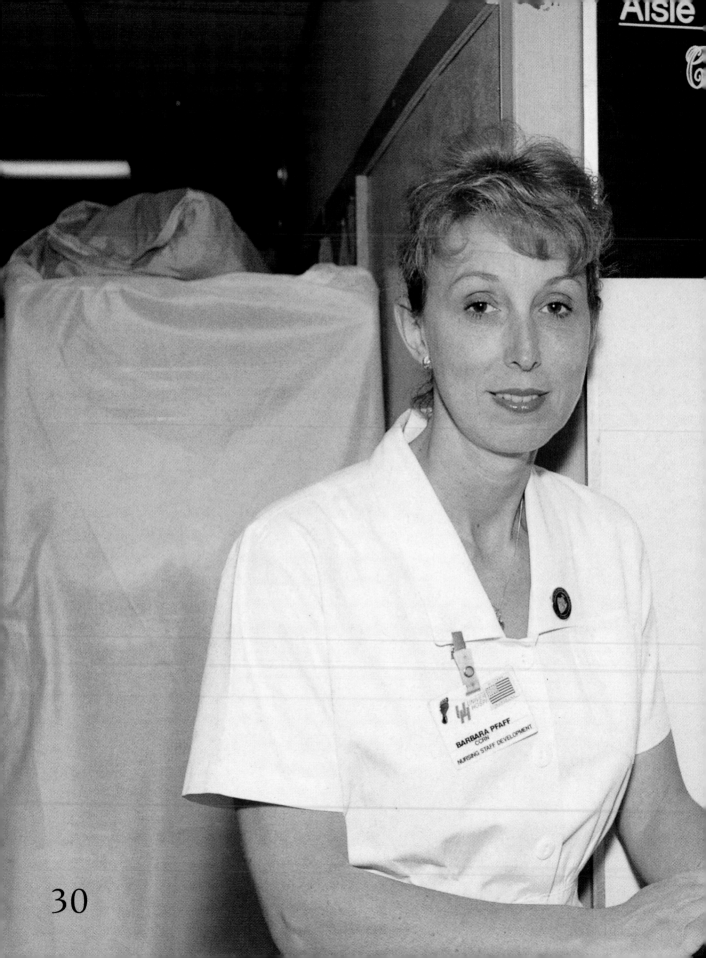

ildren's
mergency
Center

Patients who depend on her always say, "If you need something, just ask Nurse Pfaff. She'll help you!"

Meet the Author
and the Photographer

Alice Flanagan and Christine Osinski are sisters. They grew up together telling stories and drawing pictures in a brown brick bungalow in a southwest-side neighborhood of Chicago, Illinois. Today they write stories and take photographs professionally.

Ms. Flanagan resides in Chicago with her husband and works as a freelance writer. Ms. Osinski is a photographer and teaches at The Cooper Union for the Advancement of Science and Art in New York City. She lives with her husband and two sons on Staten Island.